PEP TALK

★

INSPIRATION FROM AMERICA'S GREAT COACHES

SELECTED BY
MIKE DOWDALL & SHEILA MEEHAN

CHRONICLE BOOKS
SAN FRANCISCO

★ *I dedicate this book to the three great coaches in my life: Kelly Poulos, Dennis Ranahan, and Terence Flynn.—M. D.*

To those who believe in themselves.—S. M.

A special thanks to Greg Brausen of Entertainment Marketing Corporation for his help.

Compilation copyright © 1995 by Mike Dowdall and Sheila Meehan. All rights reserved.
No part of this book may be reproduced in any form without written permission from the publisher.

Page 88 constitutes a continuation of the copyright page.

The coaches and athletes included in this book have led long careers, often with several teams.
The team listed here is the team the coach or player was affiliated with when they made their statement.

Printed in the United States of America.

Library of Congress Cataloging-in-Publication Data.

Pep talk : inspiration from America's great coaches / selected by Mike Dowdall and Sheila Meehan.
     p. cm.
  ISBN 0-8118-0542-5
  1. Sports--Psychological aspects--Quotations, maxims, etc. 2. Success--Quotations, maxims, etc.
3. Coaches (Athletics) --Quotations. 4. Athletes--Quotations. I. Dowdall, Mike.
II. Meehan, Sheila.
GV706.55.P47 1995   94-33742
796'.01--dc20   CIP

Book and cover design: Deborah Bowman

Distributed in Canada by Raincoast Books, 8680 Cambie Street, Vancouver, B.C. V6P 6M9

10 9 8 7 6 5 4 3 2 1

Chronicle Books, 275 Fifth Street, San Francisco, CA 94103

FOREWORD

BY TOMMY LASORDA

In 1954 I was playing with the Brooklyn Dodgers, and we led the National
League by 14 games. I was summoned to the office of General Manager
Buzzie Bavasi, who said he wanted to send me to Brooklyn's minor
league team in Montreal. I told him to send Sandy Koufax because he
couldn't hit a barn door with a baseball from 60 feet away. Due to a
league rule, I went and he stayed. I can honestly say it took the great-
est left-handed pitcher in Brooklyn history to send me to the minors.

In the face of adversity, I was able to maintain the self-confidence and determination that has made me a success in my profession today. I learned that you always have to believe in yourself before others can believe in you. Success is being truly happy at what you do, and I can say that I am the happiest man in the world. I proved to myself that the difference between the possible and the impossible lies in a person's determination.

This book offers words of wisdom from my peers who have helped others overcome their obstacles and achieve their goals. We all need encouragement at some point, from the President of the United

States on down to the lowest employee. Share these words with those around you and motivate them to be the best that they can be.

I believe there are three types of people in this world:

1. The ones who make it happen
2. The ones who watch it happen
3. The ones who wonder what has happened

Be Number One!

A portion of the authors' proceeds from the sale of this book will go directly to the Tommy Lasorda, Jr., Memorial Foundation.

Success is not the result
of spontaneous combustion.
You must set yourself on fire.

Fred Shero
Coach, Philadelphia Flyers

★ The only gracious way to accept an insult is to ignore it. If you can't ignore it, you try to top it. If you can't do that, you laugh at it. And if you can't laugh at it, it's probably deserved.

Leonard Patrick "Red" Kelly
Coach, Toronto Maple Leafs

★ Everybody wants to go to heaven, but nobody wants to die.

Joe Louis
Heavyweight Champion

★ You can accomplish a lot if you don't worry about who gets the credit.

> *Bill Arnsparger*
> *Assistant Coach, Miami Dolphins*

★ The taste of defeat has a richness of experience all its own.

> *Bill Bradley*
> *Forward, New York Knicks*

★ Winning isn't everything, it's the only thing.

> *Henry Russell "Red" Sanders*
> *Coach, UCLA Football*

★ Base your play on the standards most likely to defeat the champions.

Bernie Bierman
Head Coach, University of
Minnesota Football

★ Sweat is the cologne of accomplishment.

Heywood Hale Broun
Sportswriter

★ Good things happen to those who hustle.

Chuck Noll
Coach, Pittsburgh Steelers

★ I have a great deal more respect for someone who keeps coming back after losing heartbreaker after heartbreaker than I do for the winner who has everything going for him.

Wilt Chamberlain
Center, Los Angeles Lakers

★ If you send a team on the field with tears in their eyes, they can't see who to block.

Bobby Dodd
Coach, Georgia Tech Football

FRIENDSHIPS BORN ON THE FIELD OF ATHLETIC STRIFE ARE THE REAL GOLD OF COMPETITION. AWARDS BECOME CORRODED, FRIENDS GATHER NO DUST.

Jesse Owens
Gold Medalist, Track & Field

13

★ You can learn more character on the two-yard line than you can anywhere in life.

> *Paul Dietzel*
> *Coach, South Carolina Football*

★ The secret of managing is to keep the five guys who hate you from the five guys who are undecided.

> *Casey Stengel*
> *Manager, New York Yankees*

★ A fighter has to know fear.

> *Cus D'Amato*
> *Trainer, Boxing*

★ There is no virtue like winning and no sin worse
than losing.

Murray Warmath
Coach, Minnesota Football

★ If you are prepared, then you will be confident
and you will do the job. Emotion gets in the way
of performance.

Tom Landry
Coach, Dallas Cowboys

★ Coaches have to watch for what they don't want to see and listen to what they don't want to hear.

John Madden
Coach, Oakland Raiders

★ We've got too many boy scouts on this team and not enough killers.

Dick Vitale
Coach, Detroit Pistons

★ Be a dreamer. If you don't know how to dream,
you're dead.

Jim Valvano
Coach, North Carolina State
Basketball

★ I don't want to be liked. I just want to be respected.

Reggie Jackson
Outfielder, New York Yankees

★ It's not whether you win or lose, it's how you play
the game.

Grantland Rice
Sportswriter

18

CHAMPIONS KEEP PLAYING UNTIL THEY GET IT RIGHT.

Billie Jean King
Tennis Professional

★ To hell with X's and O's. If everyone in our organi-
zation is performing at a maximum level, we'll win.

Jimmy Johnson
Head Coach, Dallas Cowboys

★ Coaching is easy. Winning is the hard part.

Elgin Baylor
Coach, New Orleans Jazz

★ I'd rather have a lot of talent and little experience
than a lot of experience and little talent.

John Wooden
Coach, UCLA Basketball

★ If your work is not fired with enthusiasm, you will be fired with enthusiasm.

John Mazur
Head Coach,
New England Patriots

★ Hit your ball over the fence, and you can take your time around the bases.

John W. Roper
Pitcher, New York Mets

★ No one wants to quit when he's losing and no one wants to quit when he's winning.

Richard Petty
Auto Racing Driver

★ Always have a plan and believe in it. I tell my coaches not to compromise. Nothing good happens by accident.

Chuck Knox
Coach, Los Angeles Rams

★ Sweat plus sacrifice equals success.

Charlie Finley
Owner, Oakland A's

★ It doesn't take talent to be on time.

Peter Reiser
Coach, California Angels

★ In order to have a winner, the team must have a
feeling of unity; every player must put the team
first—ahead of personal glory.

Paul "Bear" Bryant
Head Coach, Alabama Football

It's necessary to relax your muscles when you can. Relaxing your brain is fatal.

Stirling Moss
Auto Racing Driver

★ I know how to smile, I know how to laugh, I know how to play. But I know how to do these things only after I've finished my mission.

Nadia Comaneci
Gymnast, Romania

★ Good fellows are a dime a dozen, but an aggressive leader is priceless.

Earl "Red" Blaik
Head Coach, Army Football

★ You can teach anything if you believe in it and you can understand it.

> *Ralph Miller*
> *Coach, Iowa Basketball*

★ I'm taking a day at a time. Sometimes I'm winning, sometimes I'm losing, but nothing is premeditated.

> *Joe Montana*
> *Quarterback, San Francisco 49ers*

★ The only way to make progress is to make more progress.

> *Wesley Branch Rickey*
> *Baseball Executive*

★ If the human body recognized agony and
  frustration, people would never run marathons,
  have babies, or play baseball.

Carlton Fisk
Catcher, Chicago White Sox

★ A professional fighter is not supposed to show
  the effect of a punch.

José Torres
Light Heavyweight Boxer

★ If a man coaches himself, then he has only himself to blame when he is beaten.

Roger Bannister
Miler

★ When you win, you're an old pro. When you lose, you're an old man.

Charley Conerly
Quarterback, New York Giants

★ Fame and serenity can never be bedfellows.

James Counsilman
Coach, Indiana Swimming

Risking it all makes every moment meaningful; the intensity is not something to fear or avoid, but something to relish with a rowdy grin.

Glenn "Doc" Rivers
Guard, New York Knicks

★ A champion is one who gets up when he can't see.

Jack Dempsey
Prize Fighter,
Heavyweight Division

★ Every day is a new opportunity you can build on
yesterday's success or put its failures behind
and start over again. That's the way life is.
With a new game every day.

Bob Feller
Pitcher, Cleveland Indians

★ If a coach starts listening to the fans, he winds up sitting next to them.

> *Johnny Kerr*
> *Coach, Chicago Bulls*

★ Golf is not a game of great shots. It's a game of the most misses. The people who win make the smallest mistakes.

> *Gene Littler*
> *Golfer*

★ It's bad luck to be behind at the end of the game.

> *Hugh "Duffy" Daugherty*
> *Head Coach,*
> *Michigan State Football*

★ Anytime you think you have the game conquered, the game will turn around and punch you right in the nose.

Mike Schmidt
Third Baseman, Philadelphia
Phillies

★ Never change a winning game; always change a losing one.

Bill Tilden
Tennis Player

★ Coaching is like a bath—if you stay in long enough, it's not so hot.

Clarence L. "Biggie" Munn
Coach, Michigan State Football

★ Never let hope elude you. That is life's biggest fumble.

Robert Carl "Bob" Zuppke
Coach, Illinois Football

★ Nobody owes anybody a living, but everybody is entitled to a chance.

Jack Dempsey
Prize Fighter, Heavyweight Division

THE ABILITY TO PREPARE
TO WIN IS AS IMPORTANT
AS THE WILL TO WIN.

Bobby Knight
Coach, Indiana Basketball

★ I'm going to play with harder nonchalance this year.

Jackie Brandt
Center Fielder, Baltimore Orioles

★ We are not going to play them; they are going to play us.

Henry Iba
Coach, Oklahoma State Basketball

★ The better you become, the more people will try to find something wrong with you.

Robert Lansdorp
Coach, Professional Tennis

★ If you don't invest very much, then defeat doesn't hurt very much and winning isn't very exciting.

Dick Vermeil
Coach, Philadelphia Eagles

★ You can have all the talent in the world, but if you're not interested in making full use of that talent, victory is unlikely.

George Mikan
Center, Minnesota Lakers

★ You don't save a pitcher for tomorrow. Tomorrow it may rain.

Leo Durocher
Manager, New York Giants

★ You must be aggressive, but you can't go completely nuts because you will make a lot of mistakes. It's a difficult balance.

Robert Lewis "Bob" Lilly
Defensive Lineman,
Dallas Cowboys

★ It's only a game when you win. When you lose, it's hell.

> *Hank Stram*
> *Coach, Kansas City Chiefs*

★ You have to be tough.

> *Mike Ditka*
> *Coach, Chicago Bears*

★ My attitude has always been ... if it's worth playing, it's worth paying the price to win.

> *Paul "Bear" Bryant*
> *Head Coach, Alabama Football*

Slumps are like a soft bed. They're easier to get into and hard to get out of.

Johnny Bench
Catcher, Cincinnati Reds

★ Losers have tons of variety. Champions take pride in just learning to hit the same old boring winners.

> Vic Braden
> Tennis Instructor

★ Everybody on a championship team doesn't get publicity, but everybody can say he's a champion.

> Earvin "Magic" Johnson
> Guard, Los Angeles Lakers

★ Winning makes everyone a star.

> Lenny Wilkens
> Guard, Seattle Supersonics

★ If you live sloppy, you will play sloppy. I can't
  stand it when a player whines to me or his team-
  mates or his wife or the writers or anyone else.
  A whiner is almost always wrong. A winner never
  whines.

> *Paul Brown*
> *Coach, Cincinnati Bengals*

★ Close doesn't count in baseball. Close only
  counts in horseshoes and grenades.

> *Frank Robinson*
> *Manager, Baltimore Orioles*

★ Fans don't boo nobodies.

Reggie Jackson
Outfielder, New York Yankees

★ Show me a guy who's afraid to look bad, and I'll
show you a guy you can beat every time.

Lou Brock
Outfielder, St. Louis Cardinals

★ A man's reach should not exceed his grasp.

Willis Reed
Center, New York Knicks

★ If you're a positive person, you're an automatic motivator. You can get people to do things you don't think they're capable of.

Cotton Fitzsimmons
Coach, Kansas City Kings

★ The man who can drive himself further, once the effort gets painful, is the man who will win.

Roger Bannister
Miler

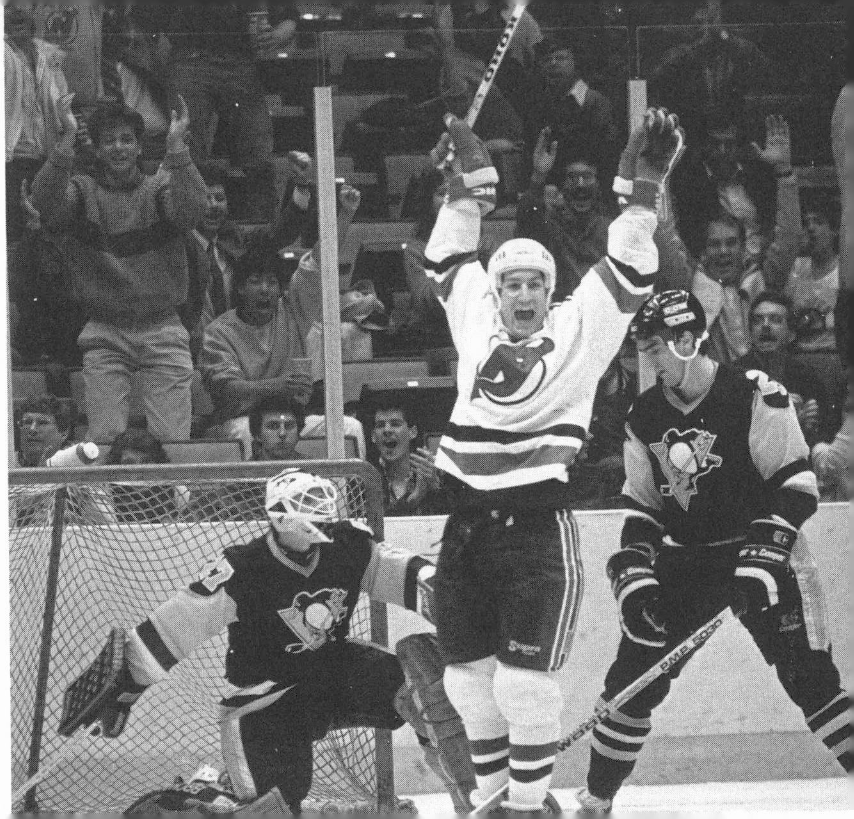

THE HARDER WE WORK, THE LUCKIER WE GET.

Vince Lombardi
Coach, Green Bay Packers

★ No matter how many errors you make, no matter how many times you strike out, keep hustling.

Tony Kubek, Sr.
Coach, New York Yankees

★ Statistics always remind me of the fellow who drowned in a river whose average depth was only three feet.

Woody Hayes
Coach, Ohio State Football

★ When all is said and done, as a rule, more is said
than done.

> *Lou Holtz*
> *Head Coach, University of*
> *Arkansas Football*

★ You're the only one who can make the difference.
Whatever your dream is, go for it.

> *Earvin "Magic" Johnson*
> *Guard, Los Angeles Lakers*

★ Winners never quit and quitters never win.

> *Vince Lombardi*
> *Coach, Green Bay Packers*

★ The bigger they come, the harder they fall.

Robert Prometheus Fitzsimmons
Heavyweight Champion

★ Fans never fall asleep at our games because they're afraid they might get hit with a pass.

George Raveling
Coach, Washington State
Basketball

★ If you are criticized, then you are important.

Doyl Perry
Coach, Bowling Green Football

★ Boys, baseball is a game where you gotta have fun.
You do that winning.

> *Dave Bristol*
> *Manager, Cincinnati Reds*

★ The horse did all the work, but Paul Revere got all
the credit.

> *Charlie Bednarik*
> *Coach, Philadelphia Eagles*

★ You don't get something for nothing.

> *Dick Butkus*
> *Linebacker, Chicago Bears*

54

Genius is perseverance in disguise.

Mike Newlin
Guard, New York Jets

★ Some people play very, very well just so they won't get embarrassed.

Lynn Swann
Wide Receiver, Pittsburgh Steelers

★ The street to obscurity is paved with athletes who perform great feats before friendly crowds.

George Allen
Coach, Los Angeles Rams

★ I can deal with the losses. It's the losing I can't handle.

Tom Runnels
Manager, Montreal Expos

★ Coaching is teaching, and it's taking the time out when a guy doesn't do it right to tell him why he doesn't do it right. Show him how to do it right.

Mike Ditka
Coach, Chicago Bears

★ A great baseball player is one who will take a chance.

Wesley Branch Rickey
Baseball Executive

Experience is
a hard teacher
because she gives
the test first, the
lesson afterwards.

Vernon Law
Pitcher, Pittsburgh Pirates

★ Class is, when they run you out of town, to look like you're leading the parade.

Bill Battle
Coach, Tennessee Football

★ It's no fun throwing fast balls to guys who can't hit them. The real challenge is getting them out on stuff they can hit.

Sam McDowell
Pitcher, Cleveland Indians

★ All I want is 100 percent and a willing disregard
for the consequences.

Howard W. "Red" Hickey
Coach, San Francisco 49ers

★ If I only had a little humility I would be perfect.

Ted Turner
Owner, Atlanta Braves & Hawks

★ Show me a good and gracious loser and I'll show
you a failure.

Knute Rockne
Coach, Notre Dame Football

★ Very simple. Nothing will work unless you do.

John Wooden
Coach, UCLA Basketball

★ The man who complains about the way the ball
bounces is likely the one who dropped it.

Lou Holtz
Head Coach, University of
Arkansas Football

★ There are two theories on hitting the knuckleball.
Unfortunately, neither of them work.

Charlie Lau
Coach, Chicago White Sox

★ Defeat is worse than death because you have to live with defeat.

Bill Musselman
Athletics Director, Minnesota

★ Serenity is knowing that your worst shot is still going to be pretty good.

Johnny Miller
Golfer

★ If you can't explain it, how can you take credit for it?

Harold "Red" Grange
Halfback, Chicago Bears

Success without honor
is an unseasoned dish;
it will satisfy your hunger,
but it won't taste good.

Joe Paterno
Coach, Penn State Football

★ Success is the best builder of character.

Adolph Rupp
Coach, Kentucky Basketball

★ Every team has a pair of top players, but it's the third man down who wins and loses games.

Del Harris
Head Coach, Houston Rockets

★ The coach who thinks his coaching is more important than talent is an idiot.

Joe Lapchick
Coach, New York Knicks

★ Keep your eye on the ball and hit 'em where they ain't.

William Henry "Wee Willie" Keeler
Outfielder, Brooklyn Dodgers

★ I don't think anything is unrealistic if you believe
you can do it. I think if you are determined enough
and willing to pay the price, you can get it done.

Mike Ditka
Coach, Chicago Bears

★ Winning is the name of the game. The more you win, the less you get fired.

Armand "Bep" Guidolin
Coach, Boston Bruins

★ As long as a person doesn't admit he is defeated, he is not defeated—he's just a little behind and isn't through fighting.

Darrell Royal
Coach, Texas Football

★ If it's your day, you can't do nothing wrong.

Jimmy Bryan
Auto Driver,
Indianapolis 500 Winner

★ Enthusiasm is everything. It must be as taut and
vibrating as a guitar string.

Pelé
Soccer Player

★ The reason we succeeded where other attempts
failed is that we are able to stand sheer tedium.

Dean Caldwell
Mountain Climber

I HATE TO LOSE MORE THAN I LIKE TO WIN.

Jimmy Connors
Tennis Professional

★ Everyone has some fear. A man who has no fear belongs in a mental institution. Or on special teams.

Walt Michaels
Head Coach, New York Jets

★ Champions, actors, and dictators should always retire when they are on top.

Juan-Manuel Fangio
Auto Racer

★ Winning is only half of it. Having fun winning is the other half.

> *Bum Phillips*
> *Coach, Houston Oilers*

★ If your stomach disputes you, lie down and pacify it with cool thoughts.

> *Leroy "Satchel" Paige*
> *Pitcher, St. Louis Browns*

★ The fewer the rules a coach has, the fewer there are for a player to break.

> *John Madden*
> *Coach, Oakland Raiders*

★ Winning is what life is all about.

Chuck Fairbanks
Coach, Oklahoma Football

★ I have an affinity for futility.

Joe Robbie
Owner, Miami Dolphins

★ Every time you win, it diminishes the fear a little
bit. You never really cancel the fear of losing; you
keep challenging it.

Arthur Ashe
Tennis professional

★ Ain't no man can avoid being born average, but there ain't no man got to be common.

Leroy "Satchel" Paige
Pitcher, St. Louis Browns

★ Winning is the thing. If it wasn't, they wouldn't keep score.

Will Robinson
Coach, Illinois State Basketball

THE BEST THING ABOUT BASEBALL
IS THAT YOU CAN DO SOMETHING
ABOUT YESTERDAY TOMORROW.

Manny Trillo
Outfielder, Philadelphia Phillies

★ If you're going to be a champion, you must be willing to pay a greater price than your opponent will ever pay.

Charles "Bud" Wilkinson
Coach, Oklahoma Football

★ Don't look back. Something may be gaining on you.

Leroy "Satchel" Paige
Pitcher, St. Louis Browns

★ The difference between the impossible and the possible lies in a person's determination.

> *Tommy Lasorda*
> *Manager, Los Angeles Dodgers*

★ Egotism is the anesthetic that dulls the pain of stupidity.

> *Frank Leahy*
> *Coach, Notre Dame Football*

★ You just have to treat death like any other part of life.

> *Tom Sneva*
> *Race Car Driver*

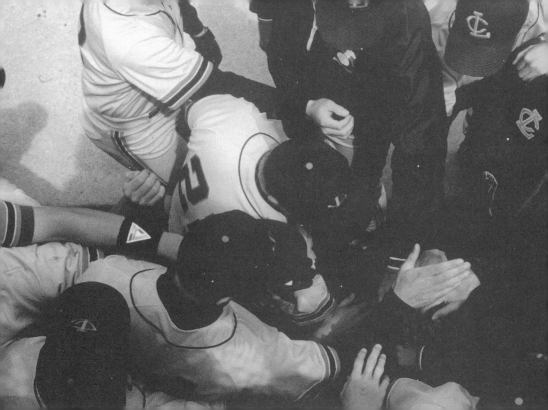

It's never over till it's over.

Yogi Berra
Manager, New York Mets

★ When you're winning, beer tastes better.

Jimmy Dykes
Manager, Detroit Tigers

★ Becoming number one is easier than remaining number one.

Bill Bradley
Forward, New York Knicks

★ Friendships are forgotten when the game begins.

Alvin Dark
Manager, Kansas City A's

★ If you always tell the truth, you don't have anything to remember.

Dick Motta
Coach, Chicago Bulls

★ I don't look for excuses when we lose, and I don't buy excuses when we win.

Dave Cowens
Center, Boston Celtics

TO SEE A MAN BEATEN NOT
BY A BETTER OPPONENT BUT
BY HIMSELF IS A TRAGEDY.

Cus D'Amato
Trainer, Boxing

Index

PHOTO CREDITS

UPI/Bettman: pp. 18, 31,
42, 48, 64–65, 70;
Reuters/Bettman: pp. 12–13,
55;
Jerry Amster/Superstock,
Inc.: p. 85;
William D. Adams/
Superstock, Inc.: p. 76;
Sportschrome West Inc./
© Brian Drake: p. 80;
Underwood Photo
Archives, San Francisco:
pp. 6, 24–25, 37, 58.